Paper Bead Crafts
7/8" to 3/4"
Paper Bead Templates

Includes 7/8"x3/4"x11" and 7/8"x3/4"x8½" Paper Bead Cutting Templates

The pages can be used as bead sheet overlay cutting templates

Designed for use with 8½" x 11" Letter Sized Paper.

Author: Julie A Bolduc

©Copyright 2021 by Julie A Bolduc

All rights reserved. No part of the book may be reproduced or transmitted in any form or by any means, electronic or mechanical, including photocopying, recording, or by any information storage or retrieval system, without written permission from Just Plain Fun.

Just Plain Fun is the Parent Company of the Paper Bead Crafts Brand and owned by Julie A Bolduc of Stratton Maine.

Contents

This book has 2 orientations, (*horizontal and vertical*) of paper bead strips of the same size. One that is 7/8" by 3/4"- 11"long and 7/8" by 3/4" , 8½" long and does not have page numbers. There are 25 copies of each paper bead template. Each template will have the strip size information printed on the center of the back of that page.

Introduction

Instructions for Use

7/8" Templates

7/8" x 3/4" x 11" Tapered Strips

7/8" x 3/4" x 8½" Tapered Strips

Back Pages

Get more information about making paper beads and read about the Author. Sources for Artwork and some Final Thoughts about this book!

Introduction

The purpose of this paper bead coloring book is to make it fun and easy to make paper beads by using templates on one side of the pages and for cutting your fancy papers into strips for making paper beads. This book is meant to be taken apart and the pages separated, so you can use the pre-drawn templates to cut your paper into strips that can be rolled up to make beads.

When you use up all of the templates in this book, you can just order another one! No need to print them out yourself wasting expensive printer ink! You don't have to worry about setting up your printer incorrectly and printing off lots of messed up sheets! The hard work has been done for you! Now all you need to do is carefully pull out the pages of this book and layer them with your decorative papers and cut away!

To remove the sheets from this book, you will need to carefully cut each page along the spine. The way to do this is to lay the open book on your table in front of you and with your hands on each side, press down hard working from the center of the book out. Then run a craft knife along the spine on the sheet you want to cut out. You can do this for each page you want to use as you need them or for all of the sheets at the same time. You will not be able to get a full 8½" x 11" sheet from this book, even though the templates are based on a sheet that is 8½" x 11", due to the margin restrictions of the book printers, there will be slight variances in the actual size of the strips.

You can still layer your book pages on your scrapbook paper and just trim around the book paper, if needed, so they are the same size, then cut along the template lines to cut your paper into strips.

This book is not intended to teach you how to make paper beads, it is intended to be another way to make beads out of paper. You should already know how to make paper beads.

If you do not know how to make paper beads, you can go to http://www.paperbeadcrafts.com and watch videos, buy paper bead rolling tools, print off bead sheets that you can design yourself and also download and print already designed paper bead sheets.

Using the Cutting Templates

To use these sheets, once they have been removed from this book, get yourself some mini binder clips. You will need 2 or three per cutting template sheet. You can get them at most office supply places.

Layer your sheets together, lining up all of the edges so they are even, place a binder clip on the opposite side of where you will start cutting. Place one on each end near the corner and one in the middle, of the same edge, for best results.

You are may want to cut off the margins before you cut your sheets into strips. (You can roll the margin strips into beads as well!) Do this with the clips on the opposite side of the margin you are cutting. You will need to move your binder clips around the sheet to keep your sheets from shifting out of alignment.

Cut your strips using your favorite method. I use a combination of my guillotine paper cutter and rotary cutter, ruler and cutting mat to cut my strips, when I use these templates. If you cut your strips using scissors, one way to keep the paper from shifting is to place 3 more binder clips on the edge next to where you will cut. Then move the binder clips to each new edge as you cut leaving the first 3, on the other edge, in place.

If you want to use paper that is bigger than 8½" x 11", you can layer the template over the larger paper lining up the edges and one corner with the larger paper's edges. Cut the large paper so it is the same size as the template, then cut your paper as you normally would. The scrap you have left over can be just cut into random sized strips or you use one of our Universal Cutting templates to mark the top and bottom of your scraps of paper.

We offer downloadable digital Universal Cutting templates, at our web site and through Etsy. If I get enough interest in these template books, I may offer the universal templates in books of their own. Let me know if you want them already printed and ready to use in book form!

Have Fun Making Paper Beads!

Paper Bead Crafts Paper Bead Template 7/8" to 3/4" 11" Long
Copyright 2021 by Julie A Bolduc of Just Plain Fun www.jpfun.com

Paper Bead Crafts Paper Bead Template 7/8" to 3/4" 11" Long
Copyright 2021 by Julie A Bolduc of Just Plain Fun www.jpfun.com

Paper Bead Crafts Paper Bead Template 7/8" to 3/4" 11" Long
Copyright 2021 by Julie A Bolduc of Just Plain Fun www.jpfun.com

Paper Bead Crafts Paper Bead Template 7/8" to 3/4" 11" Long
Copyright 2021 by Julie A Bolduc of Just Plain Fun www.jpfun.com

Paper Bead Crafts Paper Bead Template 7/8" to 3/4" 11" Long
Copyright 2021 by Julie A Bolduc of Just Plain Fun www.jpfun.com

Paper Bead Crafts Paper Bead Template 7/8" to 3/4" 11" Long
Copyright 2021 by Julie A Bolduc of Just Plain Fun www.jpfun.com

Paper Bead Crafts Paper Bead Template 7/8" to 3/4" 11" Long
Copyright 2021 by Julie A Bolduc of Just Plain Fun www.jpfun.com

Paper Bead Crafts Paper Bead Template 7/8" to 3/4" 11" Long
Copyright 2021 by Julie A Bolduc of Just Plain Fun www.jpfun.com

Paper Bead Crafts Paper Bead Template 7/8" to 3/4" 11" Long
Copyright 2021 by Julie A Bolduc of Just Plain Fun www.jpfun.com

Paper Bead Crafts Paper Bead Template 7/8" to 3/4" 11" Long
Copyright 2021 by Julie A Bolduc of Just Plain Fun www.jpfun.com

Paper Bead Crafts Paper Bead Template 7/8" to 3/4" 11" Long
Copyright 2021 by Julie A Bolduc of Just Plain Fun www.jpfun.com

Paper Bead Crafts Paper Bead Template 7/8" to 3/4" 11" Long
Copyright 2021 by Julie A Bolduc of Just Plain Fun www.jpfun.com

Paper Bead Crafts Paper Bead Template 7/8" to 3/4" 11" Long
Copyright 2021 by Julie A Bolduc of Just Plain Fun www.jpfun.com

Paper Bead Crafts Paper Bead Template 7/8" to 3/4" 11" Long
Copyright 2021 by Julie A Bolduc of Just Plain Fun wwww.jpfun.com

Paper Bead Crafts Paper Bead Template 7/8" to 3/4" 11" Long
Copyright 2021 by Julie A Bolduc of Just Plain Fun www.jpfun.com

Paper Bead Crafts Paper Bead Template   7/8" to 3/4" 11" Long
Copyright 2021 by Julie A Bolduc of Just Plain Fun www.jpfun.com

Paper Bead Crafts Paper Bead Template 7/8" to 3/4" 11" Long
Copyright 2021 by Julie A Bolduc of Just Plain Fun www.jpfun.com

Paper Bead Crafts Paper Bead Template 7/8" to 3/4" 11" Long
Copyright 2021 by Julie A Bolduc of Just Plain Fun www.jpfun.com

Paper Bead Crafts Paper Bead Template 7/8" to 3/4" 11" Long
Copyright 2021 by Julie A Bolduc of Just Plain Fun www.jpfun.com

Paper Bead Crafts Paper Bead Template 7/8" to 3/4" 11" Long
Copyright 2021 by Julie A Bolduc of Just Plain Fun www.jpfun.com

Paper Bead Crafts Paper Bead Template 7/8" to 3/4" 11" Long
Copyright 2021 by Julie A Bolduc of Just Plain Fun www.jpfun.com

Paper Bead Crafts Paper Bead Template 7/8" to 3/4" 11" Long
Copyright 2021 by Julie A Bolduc of Just Plain Fun wwww.jpfun.com

Paper Bead Crafts Paper Bead Template 7/8" to 3/4" 11" Long
Copyright 2021 by Julie A Bolduc of Just Plain Fun www.jpfun.com

Paper Bead Crafts Paper Bead Template 7/8" to 3/4" 11" Long
Copyright 2021 by Julie A Bolduc of Just Plain Fun www.jpfun.com

Paper Bead Crafts Paper Bead Template 7/8" to 3/4" 11" Long
Copyright 2021 by Julie A Bolduc of Just Plain Fun www.jpfun.com

Paper Bead Crafts Paper Bead Template 7/8" to 3/4" 8½" Long
Copyright 2021 by Julie A Bolduc of Just Plain Fun www.jpfun.com

Paper Bead Crafts Paper Bead Template 7/8" to 3/4" 8½" Long
Copyright 2021 by Julie A Bolduc of Just Plain Fun www.jpfun.com

Paper Bead Crafts Paper Bead Template 7/8" to 3/4" 8½" Long
Copyright 2021 by Julie A Bolduc of Just Plain Fun www.jpfun.com

Paper Bead Crafts Paper Bead Template 7/8" to 3/4" 8½" Long Copyright 2021 by Julie A Bolduc of Just Plain Fun www.jpfun.com

Paper Bead Crafts Paper Bead Template 7/8" to 3/4" 8½" Long
Copyright 2021 by Julie A Bolduc of Just Plain Fun www.jpfun.com

Paper Bead Crafts Paper Bead Template 7/8" to 3/4" 8½" Long
Copyright 2021 by Julie A Bolduc of Just Plain Fun www.jpfun.com

Paper Bead Crafts Paper Bead Template   7/8" to 3/4" 8½" Long
Copyright 2021 by Julie A Bolduc of Just Plain Fun www.jpfun.com

Paper Bead Crafts Paper Bead Template 7/8" to 3/4" 8½" Long
Copyright 2021 by Julie A Bolduc of Just Plain Fun www.jpfun.com

Paper Bead Crafts Paper Bead Template 7/8" to 3/4" 8½" Long
Copyright 2021 by Julie A Bolduc of Just Plain Fun www.jpfun.com

Paper Bead Crafts Paper Bead Template 7/8" to 3/4" 8½" Long
Copyright 2021 by Julie A Bolduc of Just Plain Fun www.jpfun.com

Paper Bead Crafts Paper Bead Template 7/8" to 3/4" 8½" Long
Copyright 2021 by Julie A Bolduc of Just Plain Fun www.jpfun.com

Paper Bead Crafts Paper Bead Template 7/8" to 3/4" 8½" Long
Copyright 2021 by Julie A Bolduc of Just Plain Fun www.jpfun.com

Paper Bead Crafts Paper Bead Template 7/8" to 3/4" 8½" Long
Copyright 2021 by Julie A Bolduc of Just Plain Fun www.jpfun.com

Paper Bead Crafts Paper Bead Template 7/8" to 3/4" 8½" Long
Copyright 2021 by Julie A Bolduc of Just Plain Fun www.jpfun.com

Paper Bead Crafts Paper Bead Template 7/8" to 3/4" 8½" Long
Copyright 2021 by Julie A Bolduc of Just Plain Fun www.jpfun.com

Paper Bead Crafts Paper Bead Template 7/8" to 3/4" 8½" Long
Copyright 2021 by Julie A Bolduc of Just Plain Fun www.jpfun.com

Paper Bead Crafts Paper Bead Template 7/8" to 3/4" 8½" Long
Copyright 2021 by Julie A Bolduc of Just Plain Fun www.jpfun.com

Paper Bead Crafts Paper Bead Template 7/8" to 3/4" 8½" Long
Copyright 2021 by Julie A Bolduc of Just Plain Fun www.jpfun.com

Paper Bead Crafts Paper Bead Template 7/8" to 3/4" 8½" Long
Copyright 2021 by Julie A Bolduc of Just Plain Fun www.jpfun.com

Paper Bead Crafts Paper Bead Template 7/8" to 3/4" 8½" Long
Copyright 2021 by Julie A Bolduc of Just Plain Fun www.jpfun.com

Paper Bead Crafts Paper Bead Template 7/8" to 3/4" 8½" Long
Copyright 2021 by Julie A Bolduc of Just Plain Fun www.jpfun.com

Paper Bead Crafts Paper Bead Template 7/8" to 3/4" 8½" Long
Copyright 2021 by Julie A Bolduc of Just Plain Fun www.jpfun.com

Paper Bead Crafts Paper Bead Template 7/8" to 3/4" 8½" Long
Copyright 2021 by Julie A Bolduc of Just Plain Fun www.jpfun.com

Paper Bead Crafts Paper Bead Template 7/8" to 3/4" 8½" Long
Copyright 2021 by Julie A Bolduc of Just Plain Fun www.jpfun.com

Paper Bead Crafts Paper Bead Template 7/8" to 3/4" 8½" Long
Copyright 2021 by Julie A Bolduc of Just Plain Fun www.jpfun.com

More Information

There is a vast amount of information about paper bead making on the internet. You can start at my web site at

http://www.jpfun.com. There you will find information all about making beads with paper as well as projects you can make with paper beads. There are even special projects with templates included for making ornaments, a paper bead Christmas Tree, key chains and more!

I also offer downloadable printable paper bead cutting templates such as the ones in this book except the back side of the templates do not have the fancy designs on them and the cutting templates actually are a little bit bigger. The margins on those pages are smaller than on these pages. That is really not that much of a difference when you get down to actually making your beads. I saving that feature for these print books.

You can also get cutting templates that are designed to work with electronic cutters such as the Pazzles Inspiration Vue, Cricut Explore, and Silhouette Cameo. They are in .svg, pvg and .wpc formats. These also have the smaller margin but that is for the benefit of the cutter itself, that prevents the cutter needle from ripping the paper along the edges.

There is also some Universal marking templates you can print out, cut apart and glue to the top and bottom of your fancy sheets and cut the strips from mark to mark. Those are designed to work with odd sized papers that don't fit the printers and cutters that are out there. Such as gift wrap, newspaper, magazine pages and more!

You can also go to the following Social Media Pages as well!

- You Tube: https://www.youtube.com/user/JPFunCrafts
- Facebook: https://www.facebook.com/PaperBeadCrafts
- Instagram: https://instagram.com/jpfuncrochet
- Twitter: https://twitter.com/jpfuncrochet
- Tumblr: https://www.tumblr.com/blog/jpfuncrafts
- Pinterest: http://www.pinterest.com/jpfuncrochet/

I hope you find these templates easy to use and if you have any questions, please do not hesitate to email me from my web site. There is a link at the bottom of every page that will generate an email that you can send to me directly through your own email account.

Template Sources

The cutting templates were designed with the software I use to make cutting templates for my Pazzles Inspiration Vue. I first save the template for future use as an actual machine cutting file but then I also print them to PDF for use in this book. That is the way I will be making future cutting templates for future print books.

Now that this book is in print, I actually use the templates in this book for my own beads as well.

If you like this book and are getting a lot of use from it, I would like a review on Amazon where this book can be ordered.

About Julie A Bolduc

I was born in South Weymouth Massachusetts on September 1, 1966. I have been a crafter most of my life. I started crocheting at the age of 5 years old and since then have done various types of needlecrafts including hand sewing, machine sewing, quilting, making my own clothing, knitting, cross stitch, embroidery, plastic canvas, a little painting, wood working and many other crafts to mention.

Back in 1997, when I started making paper beads, I had bought a paper bead roller called the Bead Crafter from an ad in Crafts Magazine I found. The company that made the Bead Crafter was located in Londonderry NH and has since gone out of business. To the left is the Picture of the device I used back then. I made thousands of beads using this device before the winding pin broke out of the handle.

I started paper Bead Crafts.com on August 12, 2005. I have actually been making paper beads since the winter of 1996/1997. I had a web site all about paper beads in 1997 but it did not do so well so I put it on hold and started my crochet web site JPF Crochet Club in February 1998. On February 15 1999, I registered the domain name jpfun.com. During the years from 1997 to 2005, I had done occasional Google searches for paper beads and watched the page results slowly rise over time.

I knew, in the summer of 2005 that it was time to launch my new paper bead web site, PaperBeadCrafts.com. I knew then what direction I wanted the web site to take. Instead of trying to sell already made paper beads, I decided I would dedicate the site to teaching how to make paper beads as well as what you can do with them once you make them.

The picture to the right is the set of 5 slotted paper bead rollers I offer on my site, Amazon and Etsy. I also have Adjustable Length Split Pin and Double Hole paper beads rollers. I also offer a tool for making inserting eyelets into large hole beads easier called The Bead Easy Eyelet Setter.

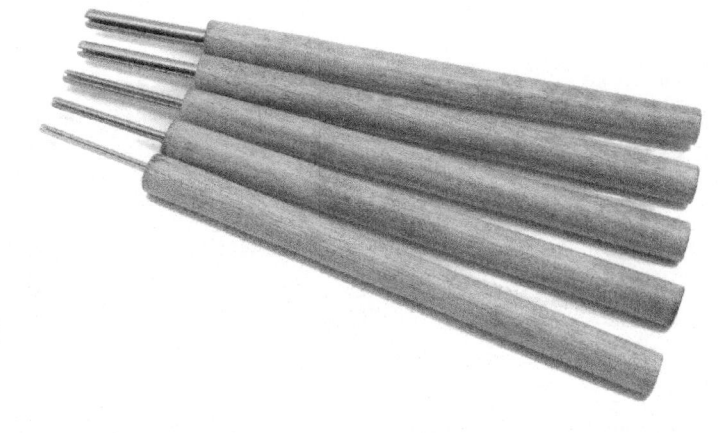

Have Fun Making Paper Beads!

Printed in Great Britain
by Amazon